HOW
HITLER
SEIZED POWER

Could it Happen in America?

JOAN FRANCIS

Lobathian Publishers
USA

Published by:
Lobathian Publishers

ISBN: 978-0-9978148-0-4

CONTENTS

CONTENTS

Never in the history of our inspired experiment in self-government has our nation been in greater danger. If we value our freedom and democracy we must understand how the German's lost theirs in 1933.

Joan Francis

INTRODUCTION

When Adolf Hitler seized power in 1933, Germany had a constitutional democracy with all the guarantees of freedom, including elected national legislature, elected state governments, legal and uncorrupted police and court systems, and a constitutional bill of rights. Yet despite these legal and institutional guarantees of freedom and democracy, Hitler was able to destroy the democratic government and establish an absolute dictatorship in three months. How did he do that? Could his tactics be used in the United States?

Though most people are fully aware of the atrocities Hitler committed *after* he seized power, relatively few are aware of the mechanisms used to bring him to power. Consequently, there are numerous deeply held beliefs about Hitler's rise to power that are simply not true. Before finding the truth, one must first peel away the layers of fiction.

First, contrary to popular belief in the United States, Hitler was not *elected*. Nor was he swept into power by his great personal popularity. Many are sure of his popularity because they remember the film footage of Hitler's speeches from a dais high above a crowd of thousands of cheering Nazis. Few realize that those were propaganda films and were shot after Hitler had seized power, and had consolidated that power. The truth is that throughout the decade of the 1920s, Hitler's party received between two and six percent of the German vote. During these years, most Germans considered Hitler some kind of nut and thought that his party, the

National Socialist German Worker's Party, (NSDAP) was an unimportant fringe party. Political rivals gave this party the nickname of Nazis, a nickname not loved by the NSDAP. They called themselves National Socialist even though their socialist platform was abandoned after Hitler took over the group. Not until the depths of the Great Depression did their vote share rise, and even then it did not rise enough to get Hitler elected.

Second, Hitler didn't use a military coup to overthrow the government. He tired that once on November 8, 1923. It was such a ridiculous and flawed attempt that, if you could forget it was Hitler, a movie about his *Beer-Hall Putsch* would play as a farce, a Peter Sellers comedy. Though the coup failed, it is important to know that from that attempt, and Hitler's subsequent trial and prison time, he learned a basic lesson that was to provide him with the true key to power. *What he learned was that no group could seize power unless they first made alliances with the national institutions of power.* The importance of this principle must be understood because everything Hitler did from 1924 until 1932 was guided by this principle.

Third, though Hitler himself was always and unquestionably anti-Semitic, it was not his rants against the Jews that brought him to power. In fact, before he achieved power he was careful where and to whom he ranted against the Jews. The truth is that Hitler, like Joseph McCarthy, had a far softer target: anti-communism. And like McCarthy, Hitler played the anti-communist card very well, using it to attack everyone left of center, including the Social Democratic party whose members were the strongest supporters of the Democracy.

Fourth, we need to deal with that old chestnut, that inflation gave rise to Hitler. You can't bring up Hitler's coming to

power without someone saying, "Oh, Germany had terrible inflation. You needed a wheelbarrow of cash to buy a loaf of bread."
What they don't say and don't know was that this "terrible inflation" existed only nine and a half months, from January 31, 1923
until November 15, 1923, which was ten years before Hitler
seized power. The runaway inflation of this nine months did in-
deed make the German Mark worthless and impact everyone in
Germany, however, it was not hard to stop. It simply took unu-
sual political courage to accomplish because it could only be
stopped by laws that hurt people who held large sums of marks,
bonds, mortgages, or bank accounts. This was done by the coura-
geous Gustav Stresemann, who was admired outside Germany as
one of his country's finest Chancellors. In Germany he was equal-
ly hated by both the left and the right.. None-the-less, he accept-
ed the difficult and unpopular task of issuing a new currency on
November 15, 1923 and ending the run-away inflation. To accomplish this, however, he had to employ the double edged
sword: The Enabling Act of Oct 13, 1923. Because Parliament
was so divided, and the left and right were so unable to co-
operate, they could do nothing, rather like our current Congress.
The Enabling Act allowed the Chancellor to execute a law without legislative action by the Parliament.

Hitler came to power on January 30, 1933. By the end of
April, he had demolished the democratic government; by the
end of the year he had consolidated his absolute tyranny. How
did he move from a comic failure in the Beer-Hall Putsch of
1923 to modern history's most abhorrent tyrant? How did he,
without a military coup and without popular support, overthrow a constitutional republic and establish an absolute dictatorship in just three months? It is of crucial importance that we

understand this because there are many frightening parallels between Hitler's methods and events happening in our politics today.

To understand Hitler's campaign for power from 1922 through 1933 we need a few clues in regard to what was happening to Germans in those years.

WHY WAS HITLER'S GOVERNMENT CALLED THE THIRD REICH?

THE FIRST REICH

Reich is a German term that means realm but implies a grand realm of an emperor or king. The first Reich is the term used for the time of Charles the Great, (Charlemagne) beginning about 800. He united Western Europe and his empire was called the Holy Roman Empire.

GERMANY'S SECOND REICH
LASTED 48 YEARS

In 1871 Otto von Bismarck, the *Iron Chancellor*, succeeded in unifying a multitude of German principalities that had been bound loosely together under the German Confederation. Under Prussian leadership, Bismarck set up a modern German Nation ruled by the Hohenzollern, the first Monarch being Kaiser William I.

In concession to a strong democratic movement in Germany, this government offered universal male suffrage to elect representatives to the government. Though true power was maintained in the hands of a well-trained bureaucracy consisting of the *Junker*, (the elite landed aristocracy) this regime was for the most part well liked and was drifting toward a British form of constitutional monarchy.

To understand how Hitler succeeded in seizing power and claiming the grandiose title of Third Reich for his government, one needs to understand what happened to this ruling power of monarch and aristocracy tempered by representative government. How did Germany come to be ruled by a short-lived constitutional democracy?

WORLD WAR I
AND THE
TREATY OF VERSAILLES

It's surprising that more Americans aren't taught this part of German history, because the establishment of a German democracy was brought about, in part, by an action of a U.S. president. Germany's first democracy was actually the result of a *regime change* demanded by Woodrow Wilson.

It was in the final year of World War I, then known as the Great War, or the War to End All Wars. The modern world had not yet learned to number their great wars. Despite the fact that no British, French, Russian, or American soldiers were on German soil and Germans soldiers were dug in all over Europe, the German military leaders, Generals Erich Ludendorff and Paul von Hindenburg believed, for several valid reasons, that Germany was about to lose the war. This fact was not obvious to the German people. However the military leadership knew their ability to continue to supply soldiers and war material was almost at an end and the entry of the United States and its men and war supplies had tilted the balance toward the Allies. Ludendorff and Hindenburg advised Kaiser Wilhelm II that Germany should seek peace before it fell to invading armies.

It was decided that Germany should approach Woodrow Wilson seeking peace terms based on the idealistic Fourteen Points for Peace speech Wilson had given before congress in

January of 1918. However, Wilson replied that he would not negotiate with the German government if "the military rulers and monarchist autocrats" remained in power.

German leaders knew that if they were left to the tender mercies of England and France, their new little nation would be torn asunder. They knew they needed Wilson and his Fourteen Points. The decision was made. They would surrender and change the ruling class of Germany.

It was one of the most amazing, peaceful and total regime changes in the history of the world. Kaiser William II abdicated and all over Germany, the old political order folded without resistance. Quietly, the princes, and kings and aristocracy who had ruled for centuries, handed over the reins of power to revolutionary committees of Social and Independent Democrats. The aristocracy's fall from power left one large *institution of power* with no love for democracy and open to be wooed into an alliance with Hitler.

A National Assembly convened in the town of Weimar. They wrote a new constitution which was adopted on 11 August 1919, creating a Federal Republic with a parliamentary democracy.

This new government became known to historians as The Weimar Republic and to Hitler and his followers as The November Criminals. Some of the people who did not believe Germany really lost the war, saw the change of power from Monarch to Republic as a conspiracy perpetrated by those who took the reins of power. This and other conspiracy theories were woven into Hitler's emotional speeches.

THE WEIMAR REPUBLIC
LASTED 14 YEARS

It could be reasonably argued that if peace had been established under the principles of Woodrow Wilson's 14 points for peace, and his speeches encouraging self-determination for all colonial possessions, the world might have avoided Hitler, World War II, and much of the current Arab hatred of the western powers. That would, however, be a debate without proofs because it didn't happen. Wilson was sent packing from Versailles. The French and English agreed to only one of his suggestions, The League of Nations, which Wilson's own congress rejected.

The elected leaders, so joyful at achieving a Democratic government, traveled to Versailles, France and assumed their first great task: negotiation of peace to end the Great War. The peace terms they were forced to sign, however, were not in alignment with Wilson's fourteen points and in fact were so unfair that they were condemned by all sides, liberals and conservatives around the world. Many observers, including Herbert Hoover and John Maynard Keynes forecast that the treaty would sow the seeds of the next great war. And sow it did.

So what were the terms of this peace settlement? In short, the Treaty of Versailles said Germany started the war, Germany lost the war, and Germany must pay for the war.

WHAT REALLY CAUSED WORLD WAR I?

In school, we are taught, (briefly) that on 28 June 1914, a Serbian, Gavrilo Princip, shot and killed Archduke Franz Ferdinand and his Duchess, Sophie. Without much further explanation we are told that this ignited WWI. If we are thoughtful, we wonder how did an assassination of an Austro-Hungarian Archduke by a Serbian lead to world war? We might also wonder how this led the delegates at Versailles to the conclusion that Germany began the war?

For the purpose of this essay, the brief answer must be that each of the countries that went to war felt themselves threatened. Austria-Hungary was afraid of Russian expansion and the Pan-Slavs, England was afraid of Germany's growing sea power, Germany feared she was encircled by France, Russia, and Britain, France found the simple existence a united Germany frightening. Russia feared the fact that she had been exposed as politically and militarily weak during the Japanese war. These fears were not entirely unfounded. Therefore all the countries had for some time been engaged in a very expensive arms race and also multiple attempts to form secret alliances and promises of mutual assistance in time of attack. The incidents that happened in the fifty years prior to 1914 had enhanced the talk of war, spurred the arms race, and proliferated the secret alliances. It left the hawks of all countries itching for a nice little war filled with valor, conquest and glory. The assassination of the Archduke Ferdinand was the match that lit the first fuse in a chain reaction of alliances.

First Austria made ten demands of Serbia. When Serbia agreed to only eight, Austria declared war on July 28, 1914. Russia ordered partial mobilization on July 29 to support Serbia. Germany mobilized on July 30 in support of Austria-Hungary and when Russia refused to stand down, Germany declared war against Russia on August 1.

Now if Germany had marched East to engage Russia it's possible the rest of the world might have allowed things to play out as a local war started by Austria-Hungary. However Germany's war plan, the Schlieffen Plan, envisioned a quick, massive invasion of France to cover their western front before marching on Russia. Per the Schlieffen plan, Germany attacked Luxembourg on August 2 and declared war against France on August 3, and Belgium on August 4. Britain responded to these acts by declaring war on Germany on August 4. Since Luxembourg, France, Belgium and Britain had not in any way been combatants in the conflict before Germany attacked, it is understandable that Versailles might accept the notion that Germany started World War I. Though all countries had been preparing for a nice little war, they were instead slogged down in the death, muck and mire of an endless war of attrition. As the war progressed there was no valor, no glory, no conquest. There was just death, sacrifice and debt. Both England and France were secretly bankrupt and the United States was calling in their loans, refusing to forgive any of the debt. Leaders of England and France could not accept any blame for the disaster. Germany would bare the blame, the shame, the debt.

GERMANY AFTER VERSAILLES

The German people had suffered World War I and with it loss of life and pride. Loss of the war and blame for war brought loss of their Monarchy and well-liked government as well as the harsh measures of the Versailles Treaty and the great financial burden of reparations. They also faced loss of jobs and stable economy. In addition, on January 10, 1923, French troops marched into the Ruhr and seized German coal and coke resources, railroads and ships. The French government claimed that this was not military operation, but a security operation to ensure delivery of reparations. Though all of Germany, Left, Right and Center, was united in outrage, the government could do nothing. With their army sharply reduced by the treaty, military action was unthinkable and passive resistance was not effective. Many German chancellors came and went in unsuccessful attempts to deal with postwar problems, foreign and domestic. With loss of the standing army, dozens of small secret or illegal paramilitary groups were organized, Left, Right, and Center. Hitler's group was the Sturmabteilung, the SA, (the brown shirts).

HITLER'S MOVEMENT

In the early 1920s when Hitler began his political career he was an unemployed soldier, joining various groups on the home front to spy for the military and report the political positions of these groups. This is how he first came to be a member of the National Socialist German Worker's Party, (NSDAP) the group that came to be called Nazis.

The NSDAP was a small fringe group which did hold socialist goals. However, after Hitler served one year of his five-year prison term for his *Beer Hall Putsch,* he was released and returned to the group. Taking over as leader, he presented them with his newly published book, *Mein Kampf,* and redirected their political efforts toward Fascism. The reason for the change is that after the failure of his coup, Hitler realized two things: 1) *No group could seize power unless they first made alliances with the national institutions of power, and 2) Power resided with the establishment whose goals were to conserve their wealth and power, not share it with the people. Socialism would not bring Hitler to power.*

Why do we in the United States believe Hitler was a Socialist? Granted, his party did have *socialist* in the name, but perhaps there is another reason also. At the end of World War II the United States was overtaken by the McCarthy era anti-communists hearings. This may not have been the best time to admit that Hitler was anti-communist or that right wing politicians bought him to power. This may also be the reason we have so little information on how Hitler seized power.

For most of the 1920's, Hitler was considered a comic buf-
foon, a mad man, who said such strident, outrageous things that
no one could take him seriously. No one believed he would ever
have any real power.

His appeal is summed up well by historian Eugene Davidson in his book, *The Making of Adolf Hitler:* "*The spinner* ...
had at long last found his calling in a narrow circle of dedicated
anti-republican, anti-capitalist, anti-Marxist, anti-Semites ... To
the vast majority of Germans he was, where he was known at all,
still a ranting absurd figure, a drummer for a political sideshow.
But for a relatively small group of people he had a mighty com-
pelling message. His fury and his hatreds, repeated as *leitmotiv*—
what much later the world would call his oratorical charisma—
were aimed at people very much like himself, 'the terrible simplifiers' who exchanged with one another easy answers to hard ques-
tions. It was a politically, culturally, and socially unsophisticated
audience ... and they subsisted on half-truths, shreds of learning,
and an unshakable belief in a world conspiracy against them ... "

From 1924, when Hitler was released from prison, until
1929, the Nazi share of the vote had remained at 2 to 6 percent.
It took the fear and the financial disaster of a great world-wide
depression triggered by the American stock market crash to make
more people look toward Hitler for answers.

And what was it he was repeating to his *"terrible simplifiers"*?
He ranted against communist and to him anyone left of center,
including the social democrats and labor unions were communist.
He ranted against all foreigners and all immigration. He railed
against Jews, but only in the appropriate districts; against capital-
ists, but only to the workers; against labor laws, but only to the
manufacturers; He criticized the government for not retaking the

Ruhr by force, he advocated suspension of reparations and rejection of the Treaty of Versailles. He called the parliament "November Criminals" and traitors to the Reich. He praised all things pure German and reiterated that all their troubles were due to conspiracies against true Germans.

His numbers climbed to 37 percent. Then his followers got an idea of what sort of man he really was. On August 10 1932 in the village of Potempa, nine uniformed SA men (Hitler's Brown Shirts) broke into the home of a communist coal miner named Konrad Pietrzuch, and in the presence of his mother, he was beaten and stomped for a half an hour until he died. The perpetrators were arrested and within two weeks, five of them were sentenced to death for political murder. Hitler fired off a telegram of solace, saying, "In the face of this monstrous verdict I feel myself bound to you in limitless devotion. From this moment on your freedom is a question of our honor. The battle against a regime under which this was possible, our duty."

The brutality of the crime horrified the rest of the country including many in Hitler's own party. From this time on, support for Hitler declined markedly. If left to his own devices, this could have been the end of Hitler's power. He might have declined to a footnote in history,

By January 1933 the Nazi share of the vote had dropped to 33 percent and was continuing to fall rapidly. The number of his followers was decreasing, but Hitler had long known that the path to power was not through the common people.

No group could seize power unless they first made alliances with the national institutions of power

What were these institutions of power and what did Hitler have to offer them? They were the military, the manufacturing corporations, the financial interests, the churches, right wing politicians, and the aristocracy. How could a mad-man with a rag-tag fringe-party possible gain the support of these groups? Easy.

THE MILITARY

The Treaty of Versailles had said the German Army was defeated when they were dug in all over Europe and not a single foreign soldier occupied Germany. Germany had a very proud military tradition and the army was the gainful employment for many. Officers were traditionally men from the aristocracy. To have their number limited was to lose their jobs, their position in society and their honor. Hitler promised to restore and re-arm the military in defiance of Versailles. Though a few officers were concerned enough about Hitler that there were rumors of a military coup but none developed. The military would make no moves against Hitler. *Alliance with power.*

GERMAN MANUFACTURING

As in the United States, much of the manufacturing was for military weapons and supplies. The treaty demands of disarmament had greatly damaged major manufacturing companies. So had the French occupation of the Ruhr. Hitler promised to restore and re-arm the military which would start the factories humming. He also promised to retake the Ruhr with all its factories and needed resources. Hitler also promised the he would outlaw labor unions and eliminate the labor laws awarding workers decent wages and hours. The manufacturing industry donated huge sums of money to Hitler and forced employees to join the

NSDAP (National Socialist German Workers Party—Nazi) or lose their jobs. *Alliance with power.*

THE CHURCHES

Hitler ranted that if the Communists, (everyone left of center) took over the country they would destroy the church as they had done after the Russian revolution. Both Catholic and Protestant churches urged their flock to support Mr. Hitler. *Alliance with power.*

Many years later, after working for the Nazis, Pastor Martin Niemöller of the Protestant Evangelical Church, realized what a mistake that had been and he wrote a poem which is now known to many. The poem begins, *"First they came for the communists."* This poem will be quoted in full toward the end of this book.

BANKS AND FINANCIAL INSTITUTIONS

There were great pressures on the Banking industry brought by reparations and the Depression. Hitler promised defiance of the reparations and offered German banks a means of recovery. On this he delivered. *Alliance with power.*

THE ARISTOCRACY, MONARCHIST, AND RIGHT WING POLITICIANS

When Kaiser Wilhelm II abdicated there were many from the aristocracy of all the former German principalities still involved in the government of Germany under the monarchy. They also had to step down. They had no love for the parliamentary government that replaced them and Hitler had only to praise German legend and tradition without promising to put them back in power. *Alliance with power.*

No one expected Hitler to gain true power but thought they could to use him and his loud, angry, violent followers to replace the current government. Right wing politicians were stymied in Parliament and wanted the NSDAP to help them against the left wing, SPD (Social Democratic Party). Pressures were brought to bear on the very elderly President Paul von Hindenburg, to appoint Hitler Chancellor. Just two months earlier Hindenburg had called Hitler a demagogue and had said that he would never appoint him Chancellor, but on Jan 30,1933, he did just that. Why?

There is no documented answer to this, though there are several possible factors. Hindenburg was said to be afraid of civil war and hoped to avoid that by bringing Hitler into the government. Others suggest that a scandal regarding Hindenburg's Neudeck family estate may have been used to pressure him. Heinrich Brüning, a past Chancellor, and others who knew Hindenburg, believed the old man was senile. This was denied by Hindenburg's son, Oskar and by right wing political leader, Franz von Papen. Of overriding importance was Papen's promise to keep Hitler under control. Papen reported to associates, "We have hired Hitler." and when challenged on this plan, he said: "I have Hindenburg's confidence. In two months we'll have driven Hitler so far into a corner that he'll squeak."

Whatever the reason for the appointment, General Erich Ludendorff accurately predicted the outcome. In a letter written to Hindenburg just two days after the appointment Ludendorff wrote: "By naming Hitler as Reichschancellor, you have delivered up our holy Fatherland to one of the greatest demagogues of all time. I solemnly prophesy to you that this accursed man will plunge our Reich into the abyss and bring our nation into inconceivable misery. Because of what you have done, coming generations will curse you in your grave."

It took Hitler just five hours after the appointment to disabuse them of the notion that they would control him.

To summarize, Hitler did not gain power by coup, or by popularity, or by election, or because of speeches against the Jews, or due to inflation. He simply made alliances with the right wing institutions of power, promising them whatever they wanted and posing as their sword against the left. They then placed Hitler in the Chancellor's office.

Who could have foreseen what he would do with that power? Strangely enough, anyone who read the Nazi writing could have seen it coming.

Early documents of intent were codified in a set of papers known as the Boxheimer documents outlining a war plan that included intent to commit high treason and murder. The Boxheimer documents were turned over the Frankfort police and were well known to the government, but no one paid much attention.

Perhaps even more pertinent to Hitler's "legal" means is this quote from Paul Joseph Goebbels. "*We come to the Reichstag not as friends, but as enemies. The National Socialist plan to use this arsenal of democracy to bring it down ... we are committed to the legality of means, not of ends.*"

These words are so important that every American should understand what was meant and how it was executed. Some of the democratic "arsenal" used by Hitler have parallels in our government today! Some are completed as law, others are waiting in the wings.

HITLER'S USES OF THE ARSENAL OF DEMOCRACY

FIRST CABINET MEETING

Hitler was then Chancellor but of a government with a deeply divided Reichstag, that is a parliament which he could not control. To Gain the control, he needed a new election and the ability to determine the outcome of that election. Within five hours of being sworn in, Hitler called his first cabinet meeting. He and Goebbels manipulated various rival party members and trapped them into calling a new election, an election that no one else wanted. In his diary, Goebbels wrote gleefully that for this election they would have all the resources of the state as well as radio, press, and no lack of money.

Resources of the state included use of the police force and the SA (Brown Shirts) to harass, beat, and arrest those running as Social Democrats and to shut down their newspaper, rallies and meetings on flimsy excuses.

In addition, Goebbels put on the largest, most extravagant electoral campaign ever seen in Germany.

Even more violent tactics were used against the Communist, than were used against the Social Democrats. With the Communist, the Nazi goals were not just to prevent them from winning seats in parliament, but rather to force them into open revolution so they might be totally eliminated. Goebbels wrote that in the plans for the fight against the "Red Terror ... For the moment we shall abstain from direct counter measures. The Bolshevik attempt at revolution must first burst into flame. At the proper moment we shall strike."

On February 27 the moment evidently came. A fire was set in many locations of the Reichstag, (the House of Parliament). Many believe that the Communists failed to take the bait and that the Nazis themselves set the fire. William Shirer writes in *The Rise and Fall of the Third Reich*, "The idea for the fire almost certainly originated with Goebbels and Goering." None-the-less a Dutch Communist named Marinus van der Lubbe was immediately arrested for the crime, though he was neither physically nor mentally capable of setting the fires. The burning of the Reichstag was proclaimed to be the beginning of the Communist revolution and trucks were immediately sent out all over Germany to find and arrest all known Communists.

The day after the fire Hitler convinced President Hindenburg to sign an Emergency Decree "for the protection of the people and the State." This decree suspended seven sections of the constitution, wiping out all civil rights in Germany. There could then be no freedom of opinion or speech, no freedom of assembly and association, no right to privacy of postal, telegraphic, or telephonic communications, no need for legal warrants, for search of persons, or their homes or businesses, no need for legal authority to confiscate property. In addition the decree authorized the Reich government to take over all state governments when deemed necessary. It imposed a death sentence for a number of crimes including serious disturbance of the peace.

With one "legal" document he stripped the people of all their constitutional rights and protections. How could this happen so easily? Why didn't other branches of government do something? Why didn't the people object? Look to our passage of the Patriot Act to understand how easily it can be done.

The next few days before the March 5 election were filled with violent police activity as Hitler used his new powers to obtain the two-thirds majority necessary for absolute control of the Parliament. When the votes were counted, however, Hitler still fell short. That was not his last move.

Next, Chancellor Hitler said that because of the Communist revolution, no elected Communist could take his seat in Parliament.

He still didn't have the necessary two-thirds majority, so he sent his men out to arrest enough Social Democrats to bring the number down to where he needed it. No real reason was needed for these arrests. There was no legal requirement of probable cause. He had the Emergency Decree. He could arrest anyone for no reason.

On March 23, in the Kroll Opera House in Berlin, this new Reichstag convened. There they were asked to pass an enabling act that turned all legislative powers over to Hitler and his cabinet for the next four years. This required a change in the constitution which required a two-thirds majority vote, which Hitler now had. The parliament voted themselves out of power and went home. Why didn't the people complain? In addition to the fact that there was now no right to free speech, and speaking out might get a person jailed, beaten or murdered, the existing do-nothing parliament had almost as low an approval rating as our current congress.

Now you know how he did it. Adolf Hitler did not seize power by coup, by election, or popularity. He was not a socialist, despite his party name. He was a fascist, an extreme right wing totalitarian autocrat. He first gained the support of the institutions of power in Germany by promising them what they wanted. Then, with their support, he corrupted and manipulated the German democracy and used elements of that democracy to destroy it. He and Goebbels were proud of the fact that they did it "legally" sort of. Do not dismiss Hitler as just a mad man. Insane, he may have been, but he was also brilliant. Germany's first republic went out, not with a shout, but a whimper.

Now let us consider whether any of Hitler's tactics could ever be used in our free, democratic United States of America.

PARALLELS BETWEEN GERMANY OF THE 1930s AND THE UNITED STATES OF TODAY

ECONOMIC

Like the Germans of the 1930s, our people today, no matter what their political view point, are in agreement that in the last thirty or forty years their relative economic level has been severely damaged. They are angry, dissatisfied and disapproving of our government. They differ only on who they blame for their depressed financial condition. Some blame too much government and too many liberal policies favoring "giveaways" to the poor and foreign born. Others blame the one percent, the wealthy and the corrupt politicians who pass laws allowing the rich to get richer and corporations to escape their full share of responsibilities to the country. There is a desire among both factions to "toss the bums out, a most dangerous desire for our democracy. Someone might come along who would oblige that desire.

When Germany was at this point it was easy for Hitler, with his strong-man image, to supplant the legislature with dictatorship, claiming he would sweep aside the stagnation and bring better times. There was a resignation among the people that almost anything was better than the continued bickering and useless parliament. Our current congressional leaders really should consider this.

POLITICS

Our representatives, as divided and angry as the members of the German Reichstag, are just as incapable of governing, just as incapable of compromise and legislative action as was the Reichstag. We the people seem to have no authority over our representatives to demand they do their job.

Hitler used force to corrupt the elections to get what he wanted. Two of our presidential elections have had serious allegations of fraud that were never fully investigated. Many of our states are currently passing laws which limit access to the right to vote. A few computer security experts claim that using computerized voting machines make it easy to corrupt the results out of sight of the public. Are our elections still free and valid?

THE ARSENAL
OF DEMOCRACY
AND ITS USES

THE ENABLING ACT

In order to get something accomplished in difficult or emergency situations, the German Reichstag passed several enabling acts, which were usually limited in time or purpose. These allowed various Chancellors to pass bits of legislation without taking them to the parliament. For instance, in 1923 it allowed Gustav Stresemann to issue new currency to end the disastrous problem of hyperinflation. Such an act would never have passed the deeply divided parliament.

This type of action was not invented by Hitler, but was an established action with many legal precedents. It was used many times for the good of the country. This is an example of what Goebbels meant when he said that they would use the arsenal of democracy to bring it down. First, Hitler used the tool of *state powers* including *police power* to corrupt an *election* and establish a legislature favorable to his ends. He then had this gerrymandered Reichstag pass an *enabling act* which gave him and his council all legislative power. This gave him dictatorial legislative powers.

OUR OWN ENABLING ACT

Our country has long used a similar device. We call them Executive Orders and Presidential Proclamations. These are not defined in the Constitution or by Congress, but have been justified as implied powers of Article II of the Constitution. They have been used throughout our history by all presidents from George Washington to the present. Many of them have covered subjects too controversial to pass in the legislature such as Lincoln's Emancipation Proclamation and Truman's integration of the armed forces. Yet once published, they have the force and effect of law. They become a legislative act performed by the executive branch with important implications regarding separation of powers. Unlike the German Enabling acts, these presidential acts do not require an act of Congress to enable the presidents. He acts under implied constitutional authority and it is up to Congress and Judicial branch to check actions they find over-reach his authority. No President has used them to set up a dictatorship ... yet. These acts are simply a part of that "arsenal of democracy" and the dangers of manipulation of these tools means that we, the people, and our elected representatives and courts have an ongoing duty to be vigilant and safeguard our democracy. How? There is no easy answer. Perhaps it is time for a constitution change that would define these tools. That would require a working, cooperative legislature.

OUR REICHSTAG FIRE AND EMERGENCY DECREE

Our response to the terrorist attack of September 11, 2001 was to pass the Patriot Act, which is as dangerous to our freedom and civil rights as Hitler's emergency decree following the Reichstag Fire. However, no one is worried because we all know that our security agencies are all good guys who only go after the bad guys. So we don't worry if this law eliminates the need for probable cause and judicial discretion over warrants. We feel safe if all a federal officer needs to do is say that a warrant is needed in an ongoing national security investigation. We are unconcerned if we lose all expectation of privacy and civil rights. It's not a problem if Federal agents can enter with no warning and no warrant, search our home or business without specifying what they are looking for or why. Only bad guys need to worry if federal officers can seize anything they want without ever telling you and without due process of law. Don't worry if the Patriot Act has overthrown laws against domestic spying because everyone knows spies are bad guys, so it's ok. Tell your friends that it's ok if everyone you have ever known can be under surveillance and investigation without probable cause and without a specific court order, if every phone number you call, every email you send can be intercepted and the person receiving it can be added to the investigation without ever knowing it. Since federal agents would never go after an innocent person, one doesn't need to be concerned if agents can set up a trap on any ISP and the service must T R U S T the agent to take only information on bad guys. There is no danger to law abiding citizens if agents can issue a roving warrant or National Security Letter in any place they think you might use, an internet café, a library, or a college campus. Anyone served with such a demand must comply and can't even disclose the order has been issued. You needn't be concerned if they can demand your financial records, health records, school records, or library borrowing records. We all know that in our American democracy, none of this material would ever be used for a bad purpose, only to catch terrorists. After all, we are not Germany of the 1930s and our presidential candidates are not Hitler.

The weaknesses in democracy that Hitler and Goebbels saw in the Weimar Republic and called the *"arsenal of democracy,"* are all available in our country as well. Much of the protection from tyranny built into our Bill of Rights has been negated by the Patriot Act. The dissatisfaction of the people with their government, the lack of an effective legislative body and the possibility of legislation enacted by the executive branch all leave our country vulnerable to any person obsessed with power. We must be very careful who we chose in the next election.

For those in the United States who believe democracy is a spectator sport or perhaps some other guys job, here is the poem by Pastor Martin Niemöller of the Protestant Evangelical Church in Germany. At first he thought Hitler was the answer. When he realized that was a mistake, he tried to work against Hitler and of course, Niemöller ended up in prison. This is his poem:

First they came for the communist, and I did not speak out—
because I was not a communist;

Then they came for the socialist and I did not speak out—
because I was not a socialist;

Then they came for the trade unionist and I did not speak out —
because I was not a trade unionist;

Then they came for the Jews and I did not speak out—
because I was not a Jew;

Then they came for me—
and there was no one left to speak out.

• • •

Finish this updated version of the poem for yourself:
First they came for the Terrorists

AUTHOR NOTE

As a history major in college, I learned just enough about Hitler to know I hadn't learned how he seized power and that most people I knew, held beliefs about Hitler's ascent to power that were false.

Much later in life, I had time and curiosity enough to try to find the answer myself. How did Hitler seize power? As my collection of books on the subject grew so did my concern about our democracy.

At the time I was a licensed private investigator and was writing novels featuring my private eye protagonist, Diana Hunter. Compelled to write something of the answers I had discovered, I decided to drop Diana on a page where she is falsely accused of terrorist activities and is faced with the awesome powers of the Patriot Act. She soon realizes that the source of her trouble is the fact that she is sole heir of her Great Uncle, Bennett Hunter. To extricate herself she must learn what Bennett had done and why his enemies are after her. The book became two stories, one of Diana in the United States in current time and one of Bennett in Germany in the 1930s. Chapters were interwoven and offer illumination of the two realities.

If you are curious enough to walk on the streets of Germany while Hitler was coming to power, or explore this country under the Patriot act, you might like to read the book, *Silent Coup*.

If you would like to delve deeper into German history, I have included a bibliography of the books I found in the hunt for answers.

ABOUT THE AUTHOR

Joan Francis graduated from the University of Washington in Seattle with a BA. Her major was History. She has had four different careers. She worked as a Librarian, a Newspaper Reporter, a Licensed Private Investigator, and writer. She has written four novels featuring private investigator, Diana Hunter. Her novels are *Old Poison*, *Corporatocracy Rules*, *Silent Coup*, and *Deadly Treasure*. All are available online.

BIBLIOGRAPHY

The following books were helpful in understanding *How Hitler Seized Power*:

Allen, William Sheridan. *The Nazi Seizure of Power: The Experience of a Single German Town 1930 – 1935*. Chicago: Quadrangle Books, 1965. Print.
> **NOTE:** For this wonderful book, Allen lived in a town in Central Germany, did extensive documentary research and in-depth interviews with the people. It allows the reader the experience true understanding how it could happen.

Engelmann, Bernt. *In Hitler's Germany: Everyday Life in the Third Reich*. New York: Pantheon Books, 1988. Print.
> **NOTE:** This is one of my favorite books. It is a memoir showing how everyday people survived and lived under Hitler.

Evans, Richard J. *The Coming of the Third Reich*. New York: Penguin Books, 2005. Print.

Flood, Charles Bracelen. *Hitler: The Path to Power*. Boston: Houghton Mifflin, 1989. Print.

Davidson, Eugene. *The Making of Adolf Hitler: The Birth and Rise of Nazism*. New York: Macmillan Publishing Company, Inc., 1977. Print.
> **NOTE:** Very useful text.

Kershaw, Ian. *Hitler: 1889 – 1936 Hubris*. New York: W.W. Norton & Company, 1999. Print.
> **NOTE:** Very useful text.

Nicholls, Anthony J. *Weimar and the Rise of Hitler*. 2nd ed. New York: St. Martin's Press, 1980. Print.

Shirer, William L. *The Rise and Fall of the Third Reich: A History of Nazi Germany.* New York: Simon and Schuster, 1960. Print.

Guerin, Daniel. *The Brown Plague: Travels in Late Weimar and Early Nazi Germany.* Durham: Duke University Press, 1994.

• • •

The following books were of general interest regarding this period of history:

Allen, Charles R. Jr. *Heusinger of the Fourth Reich: The Step-By-Step Resurgence of the German General Staff.* New York: Marzani & Munsell, 1963. Print.

Black, Edwin. *IBM and the Holocaust. The Strategic Alliance between Nazi Germany and America's Most Powerful Corporation.* New York: Crown Publishers, 2001. Print.

Blandford, Edmund. *Under Hitler's Banner: Serving the Third Reich.* Ramsbury, UK: Airlife Publishing Ltd, 1996. Print.

Breuer, William B. *Unexplained Mysteries of World War II.* Hoboken, NJ: Castle Books, 2008. Print.

Childers, Thomas. *A History of Hitler's Empire.* Chantilly, VA: The Teaching Company, 2001. Print.

Coole, W. W. and Potter, M. F., ed. *Thus Spake Germany.* London: G. Routlege & Sons Ltd, 1941. Print.
> NOTE: An interesting and disturbing book. Written in the depths of World War II and within memory of WW I. If you want a work that casts all blame for both wars on the German character, this would be your book.

Creighton, Christopher. *Op. JB: The Last Great Secret of the Second World War.* New York: Simon Schuster Trade, 1996. Print.
> NOTE: Publisher's note says Simon & Schuster could not " ... verify his account by independent research ... " and that " ... readers will have to make their own judgments ... "

Farago, Ladislas. *The Game of the Foxes: The Untold Story of German Espionage in the United States and Great Britain During World War II*. New York: Hodder & Stoughton, 1971. Print.

Friedhoff, Herman. *Requiem for the Resistance: The Civilian Struggle Against Nazism in Holland and Germany*. London: Bloomsbury Pub Ltd, 1989. Print.

Gay, Peter. *My German Question: Growing Up in Nazi Berlin*. Cambridge: Yale University Press, 1998. Print.

Gill, Anton. *An Honourable Defeat: A History of German Resistance to Hitler, 1933 – 1945*. New York: Henry Holt and Company, 1994. Print.

Graber, Gerry. *Stauffenberg*. New York: Ballantine Books, 1973. Print.

Harrington, Dale. *Mystery Man: William Rhodes Davis: Nazi Agent of Influence*. Dulles, VA: Brassey's, 1999. Print.

Haufler, Hervie. *The Spies Who Never Were: The True Story of the Nazi Spies Who Were Actually Allied Double Agents*. New York: NAL Trade, 2006. Print.

Higham, Charles. *Trading With the Enemy: An Exposé of the Nazi American Money Plot, 1933 – 1949*. New York: Dell Publishing Company, 1983. Print.

Hillel, Mark and Henry, Clarissa. *Of Pure Blood*. New York: McGraw-Hill, 1976. Print.

Höhne, Heinz. *The Order of the Death's Head: The Story of Hitler's SS*. London: Penguin Books, 1966. Print.

Hughes, Matthew & Mann, Chris. *Inside Hitler's Germany: Life Under the Third Reich*. New York: MJF Books, 2000. Print.

Infield, Glenn B. *The Secrets of the SS*. New York: Jove, 1982. Print.

Kilzer, Louis. *Hitler's Traitor. Martin Bormann and the Defeat of the Reich*. Novato, CA: Presidio Press, 2000. Print.

Kippenhahn, Rudolf. *Code Breaking: A History of Exploration*. New York: The Overlook Press, 2000. Print.

Kirkpatrick, Sidney D. *Hitler's Holy Relics: A True Story of Nazi Plunder and the Race to Recover the Crown Jewels of the Holy Roman Empire*. New York: Simon & Schuster, 2010. Print.

Knoke, Heinz. *I Flew for the Fuhrer*. New York: Henry Holt and Company, 1953. Print.

Kross, Peter. *The Encyclopedia of World War II Spies*. Fort Lee, NJ: Barricade Books, 2001. Print.

LeBor, Adam and Boyes, Roger. *Seduced by Hitler: The Choices of a Nation and the Ethics of Survival*. New York: Barnes & Noble Books, 2005.

Loftus, John. *The Belarus Secret*. New York: Alfred A. Knopf, 1982. Print.

Manz, Bruno. *A Mind in Prison: The Memoir of a Son and Soldier of the Third Reich*. Washington, D.C.: Brassey's, 2000.

Rodgers, William. *Think: A Biography of the Watsons and IBM*. New York: Stein and Day, 1969.

Shirer, William L. *Berlin Diary (1934 – 1941)*. New York: Popular Library, 1961. Print.

Simpson, Christopher. *Blowback: America's Recruitment of Nazis and Its Effect on the Cold War*. New York: Weidenfeld & Nicolson, 1988. Print.
    NOTE: Little known and most interesting information.

Snyder, Louis L. *Encyclopedia of the Third Reich*. Kent, UK: Wordsworth Edition Chatham, 1998. Print.

Stevenson, William. *The Bormann Brotherhood*. New York: Bantam, 1974. Print.

Vassiltchikov, Marie. *Berlin Diaries, 1940 – 1945*. New York: Vintage Books, 1987. Print.

Vincent, Isabel. *Hitler's Silent Partners Swiss Banks, Nazi Gold, and the Pursuit of Justice*. New York: William Morrow and Company, 1997. Print.

Wheal, Elizabeth-Anne; Pope, Stephen; and Taylor, James. *A Dictionary of the Second World War*. New York: Peter Bedrick Books, 1990. Print.

Ziemke, Earl. *The Battle for Berlin: End of the Third Reich*. New York: Ballantine Books, 1968.

www.ingramcontent.com/pod-product-compliance
Lightning Source LLC
Chambersburg PA
CBHW060627030426
42337CB00018B/3245